PROPERTY OF
FREDERICKSBURG CITY SCHOOLS

Dragonflies

Adapted from an idea by Yasuo Suzuki
Illustrated by Yoshitaka Moriue
Consultant for English language version: Ralph Whitlock

Wayland

Look!

Dragonflies live by rivers, lakes and ponds. They fly on warm summer days.

Dragonflies spend much of their lives on or under water. These two adult dragonflies on the right have just mated. Now the female is going to lay her eggs on the stem of the water-plant.

Here you can see four eggs stuck to a stem

This ugly creature crawling down the stem is a dragonfly larva

This is an older dragonfly larva getting ready to crawl up to the air to become a chrysalis

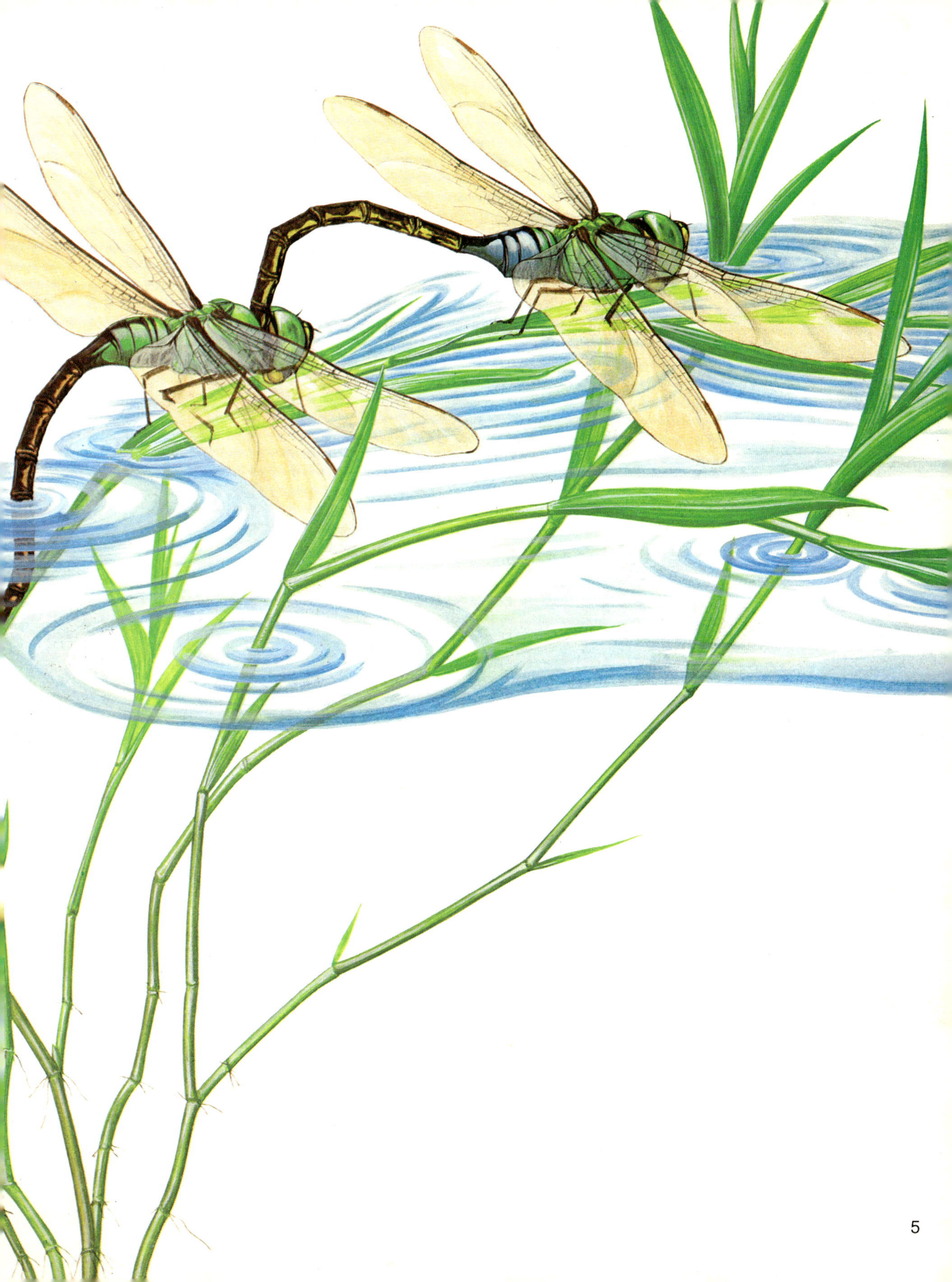

A dragonfly starts life as an egg, then becomes a larva, then a chrysalis, and finally an adult insect.

The dragonfly larva is growing big and fat. It eats many small red worms and even tiny fish. Sometimes dragonfly larvae are themselves eaten by larger fish.

This larva is crawling out of the water before it turns into a chrysalis

This adult dragonfly is hatching from a chrysalis perched on a stone

This is how a dragonfly breaks out of its chrysalis. It takes about two hours. It usually happens between midnight and dawn.

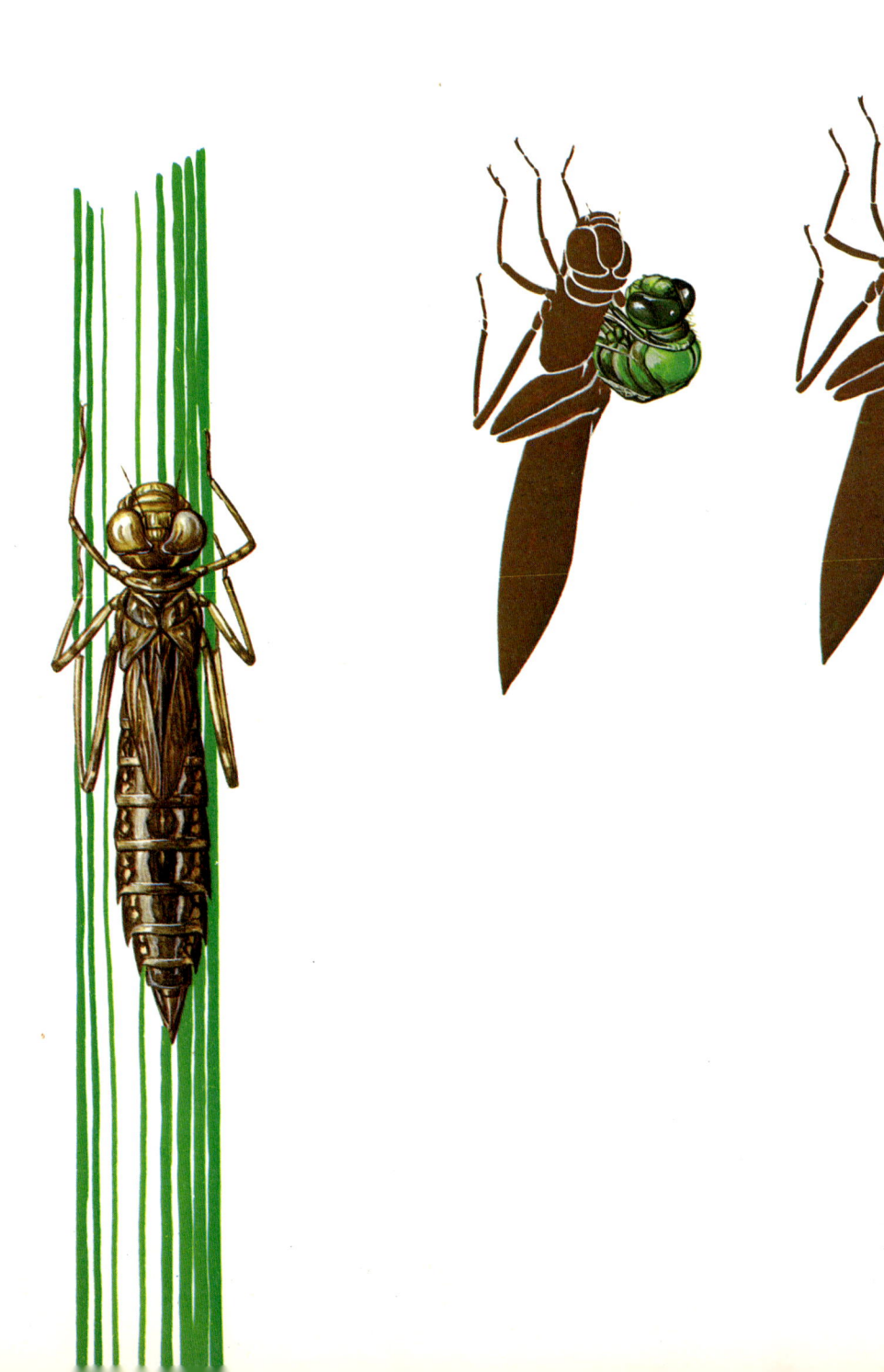

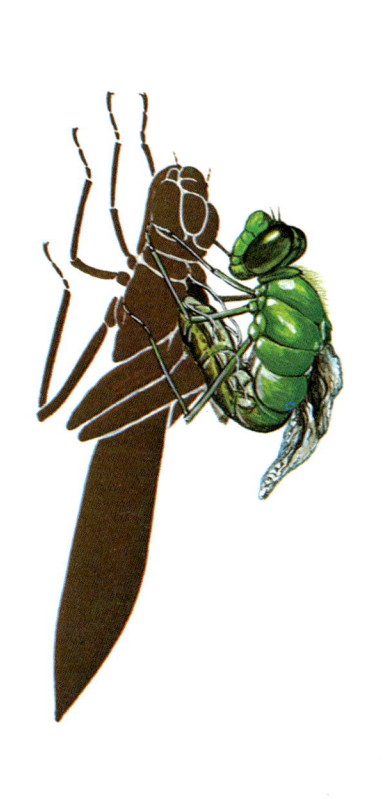

After the dragonfly is out of its shell, it has to wait about two hours for its wings to dry.

10

Then away it goes sunlight.

But s
one

Adult dragonflies are beautiful insects, with bright colours and flashing wings. They fly about in the woods and fields, skimming low over the surface of ponds and rivers.

metimes they meet danger. Here, as been caught in a spider's web.

13

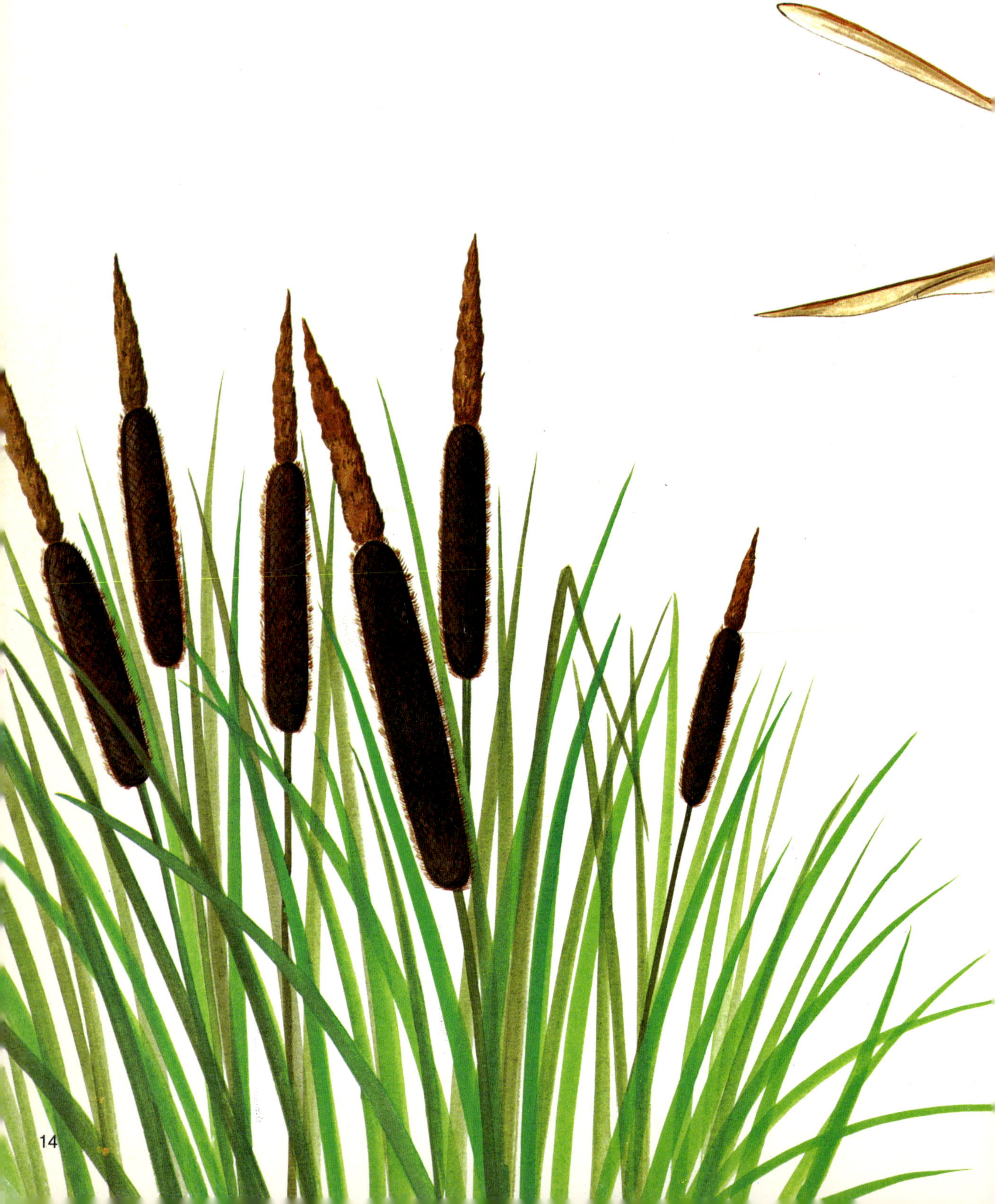

Back to the water again. It is time for this male dragonfly to find a mate.

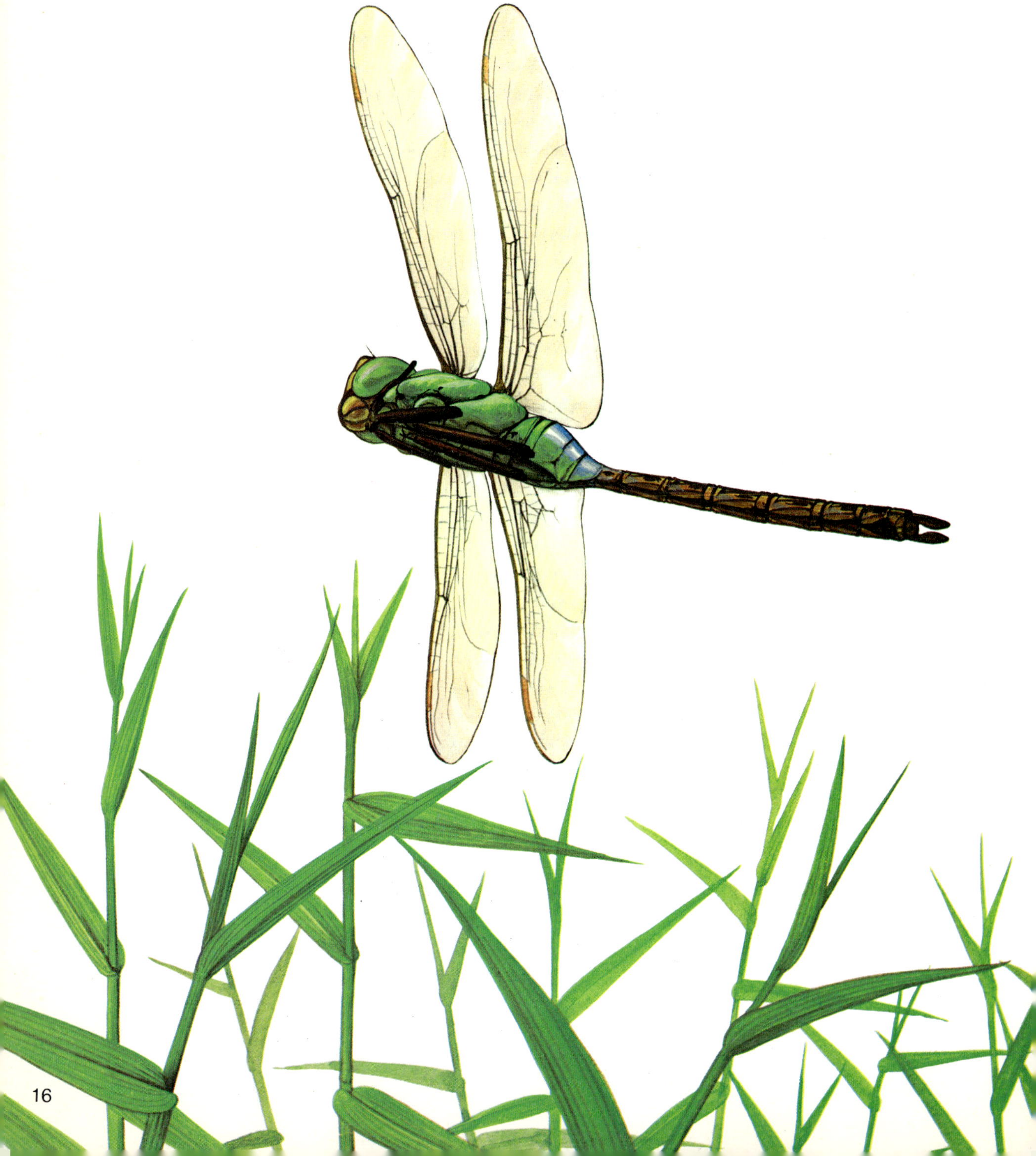

The dragonfly flies to and fro over a part of the river or lake he has chosen. If another male comes along, he drives him away.

17

A dragonfly can see small things better than we can, such as these gnats. That is because his two big eyes are made up of thousands of smaller eyes. He can also see in all directions at once.

These huge 'compound' eyes of the dragonfly are made up of as many as 20,000 or 30,000 smaller eyes. Dragonflies need to see well to be able to catch horseflies and mosquitoes, which also have good sight. No wonder it is hard to catch a dragonfly.

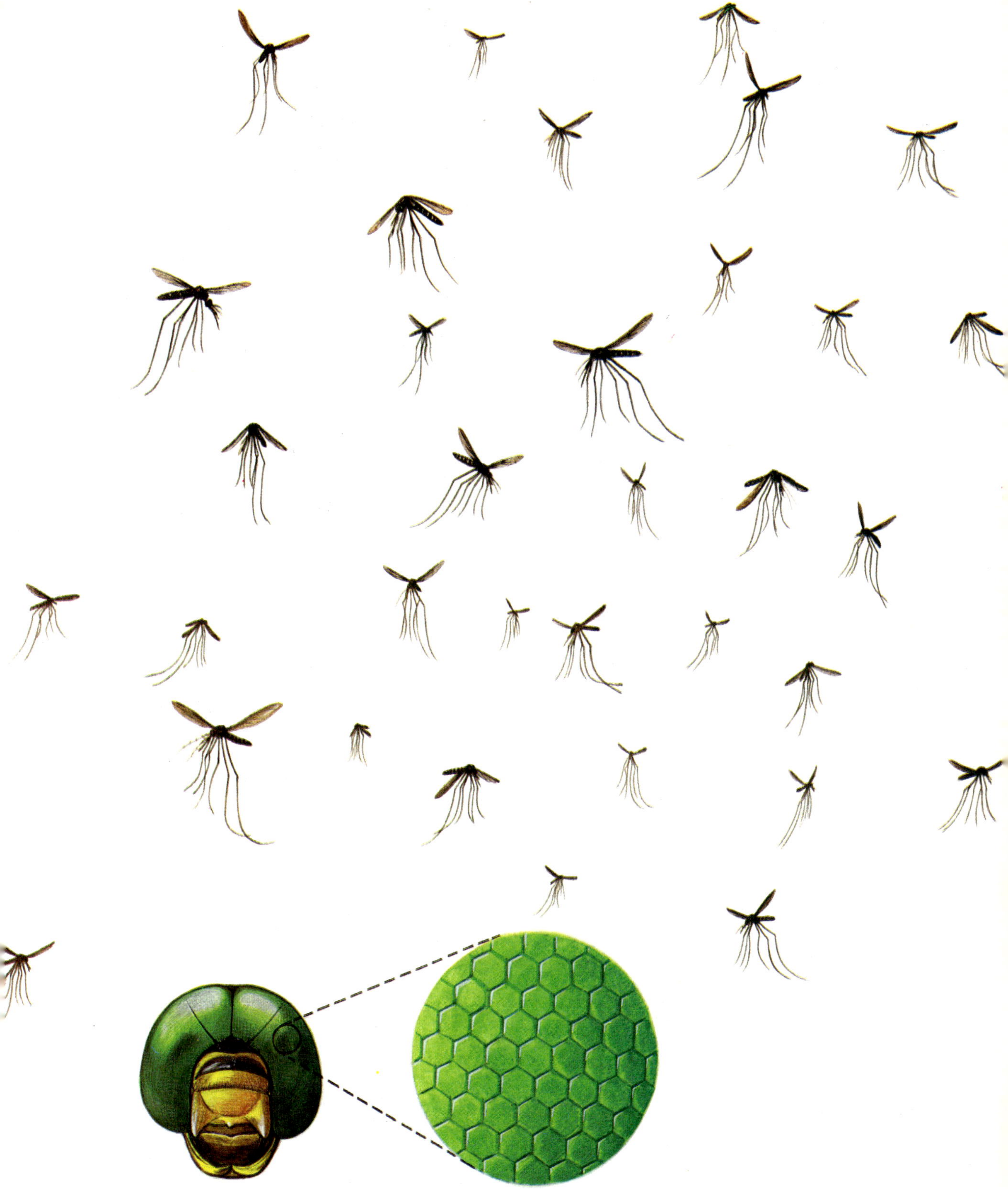

This dragonfly has just caught his dinner. It is a mosquito, like those flying around.

See how he bends his legs to form a basket, so that the mosquito cannot escape.

21

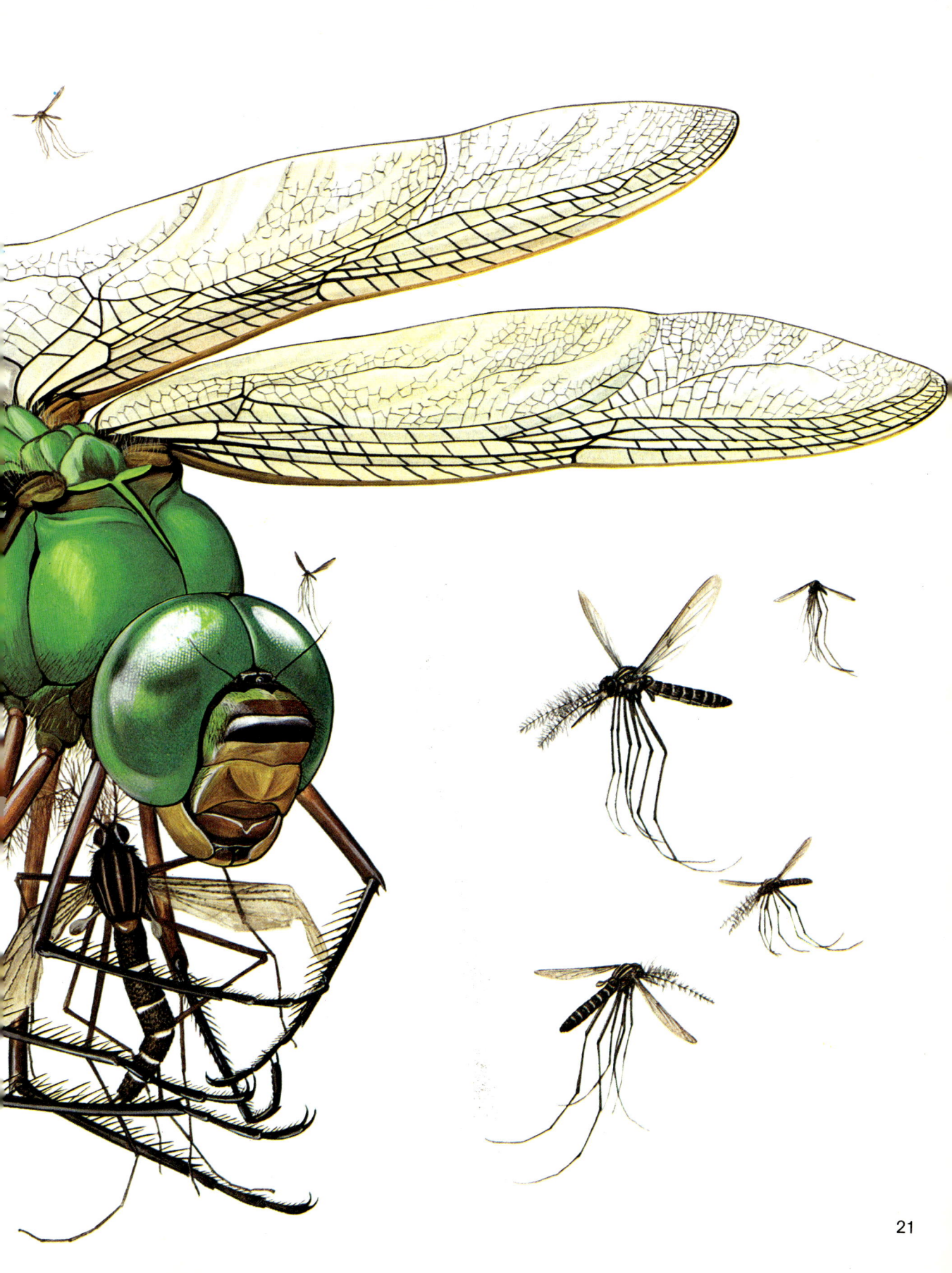

Some dragonflies, like this one, land with their wings spread. Others fold them when they land.

This dragonfly still has its wings spread, though it is just going to land.

This one has safely landed and has folded its wings.

This male dragonfly has found a mate.
Here they go, flying tandem.

The male is in front. He is holding the
female's neck by his tail, which is shaped
like a pair of scissors.

25

Here are three dragonfly larvae—small, medium and large. These pictures are just twice the real size of the insects.

There are 43 kinds of dragonfly living in Britain. The pictures on the opposite page are all the real size of dragonflies. All dragonflies have bright colours which flash in sunlight.

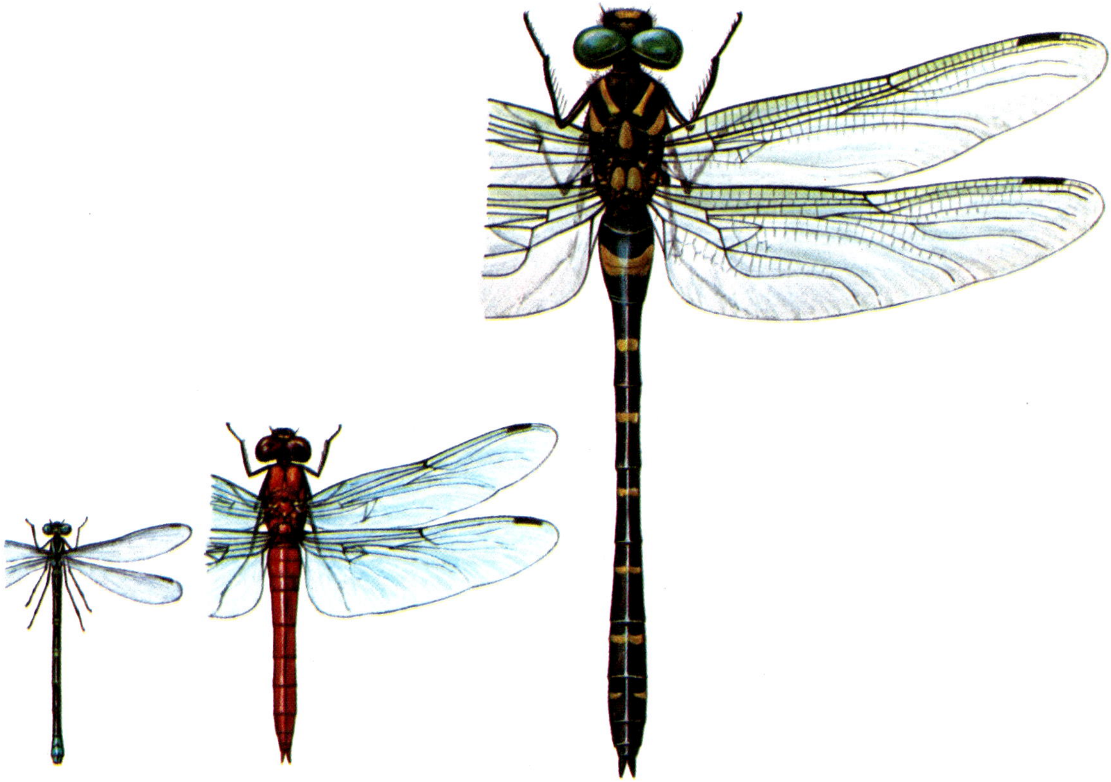

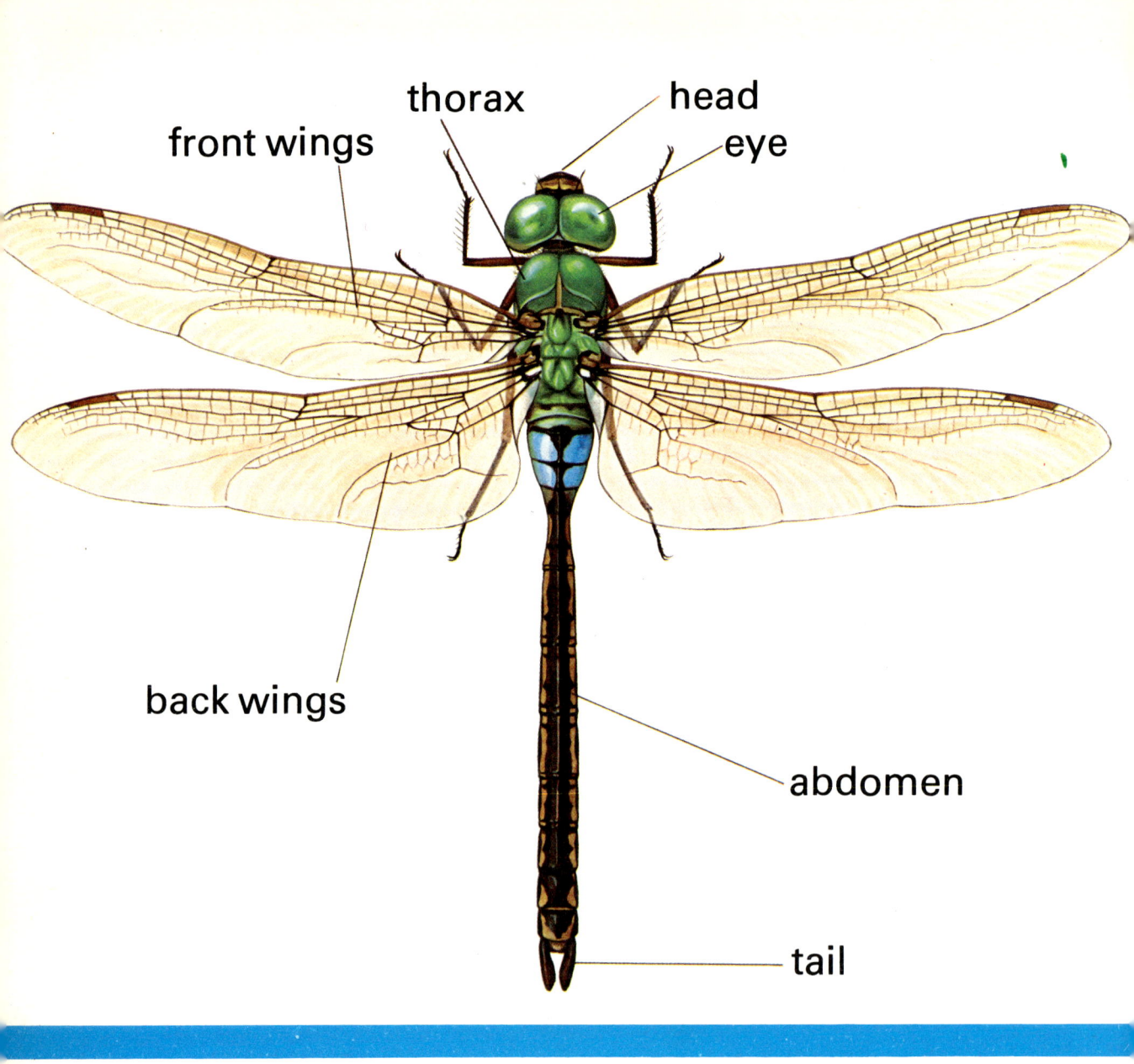

thorax head
front wings eye
back wings
abdomen
tail

Dragonflies have big heads with very large eyes but very narrow necks. The front wings are attached to one part of the body, the back wings to another part, so that the wings do not all have to beat together. That helps the dragonfly to fly backwards when it wants to. Each type of dragonfly has its own special pattern on its wings.

antenna

front leg mouth middle leg back leg

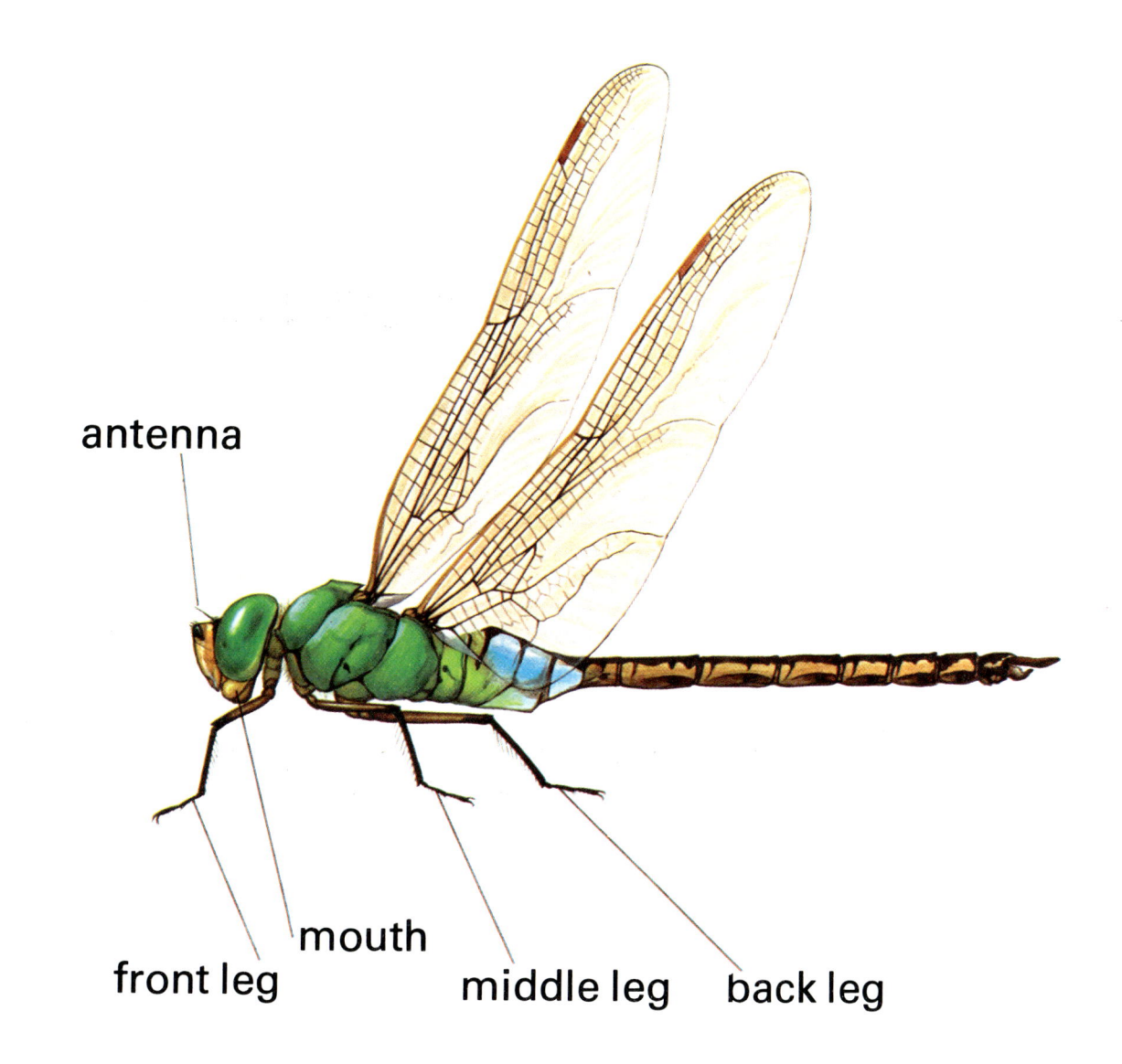

Both adult and larva dragonflies are very hungry creatures. They eat large numbers of other insects. Many of these insects (such as mosquitoes) harm us, so we think of dragonflies as very useful creatures. Sometimes ponds are made as breeding places for dragonflies, so that there are plenty of them to eat harmful insects.

These are the bodies of the male and female dragonflies. After mating in summer or autumn, the female lays her eggs, but the eggs do not hatch until the spring. The larva dragonfly, which is also known as a 'nymph', spends one or two years under the water, before climbing to the surface to become a chrysalis. It feeds on all kinds of water creatures and is very greedy.

ISBN 0 85340 538 7

Copyright © 1976, 1979 by Froebel-Kan Ltd., Tokyo
First published in English in 1979 by
Wayland Publishers Limited
49 Lansdowne Place, Hove,
East Sussex BN3 1HF, England

Printed in Italy
Phototypeset by Granada Graphics